Introduction to US Cybersecurity Careers

Introduction to US Cybersecurity Careers

Henry Dalziel

ELSEVIER

AMSTERDAM • BOSTON • HEIDELBERG
LONDON • NEW YORK • OXFORD • PARIS
SAN DIEGO • SAN FRANCISCO
SINGAPORE • SYDNEY • TOKYO

Syngress is an Imprint of Elsevier

SYNGRESS.

Syngress is an imprint of Elsevier
225 Wyman Street, Waltham, MA 02451, USA

British Library Cataloguing-in-Publication Data
A catalogue record for this book is available from the British Library

Library of Congress Cataloging-in-Publication Data
A catalog record for this book is available from the Library of Congress

ISBN: 978-0-12-802722-6

For information on all Syngress publications
visit our website at http://store.elsevier.com/

Working together
to grow libraries in
developing countries

www.elsevier.com • www.bookaid.org

TABLE OF CONTENTS

AUTHOR BIOGRAPHY

Henry Dalziel is a serial education entrepreneur, founder of Concise Ac Ltd, online cybersecurity blogger, and e-book author. He writes for the blog "Concise-Courses.com" and has developed numerous cybersecurity continuing education courses and books. Concise Ac Ltd develops and distributes continuing education content (books and courses) for cybersecurity professionals seeking skill enhancement and career advancement. The company was recently accepted onto the UK Trade & Investment's (UKTI) Global Entrepreneur Programme (GEP).

As a resource to helping you find a job in cybersecurity this book contains lots of links to internships and other employment opportunities. Please note that owing to the dynamic nature of the Internet some HTML links published in this book might be outdated. Please refer to our online resource that is available to all readers: https:// breakingintocybersecurity.com/ which contains valid working links (that are checked daily). If prompted for a password to view the material, please enter the word "concise" (without the apostrophes).

CHAPTER *1*

US Cybersecurity Jobs

Information security, or cybersecurity as it is often referred to, is a growing and exciting global industry. Our adversaries (which include state-sponsored "hackers") are determined, intelligent, and increasingly resourceful at being able to disrupt our computer systems and networks. Combating the relentless cyber threat represents an enormous challenge for the US Government and private sector enterprises since the ramifications of inaction or incompetence are devastating. Consider this: 552 million identities were stolen in 2013 due to cyber breaches![1]

US cybersecurity jobs are well paid, and as we will shortly discover, they are in high demand. Central to this book is an unequivocal fact: The demand for cybersecurity professionals is outpacing supply in both the public and private sectors.

This book works on the assumption that you are, or have recently completed some form of formal further education in an IT-related subject and are keen to work in the field, that is, you want to be an active cybersecurity professional testing and patching networks and computer systems. We also assume that you are now looking to take the next step and start building your cybersecurity career. (Although we assume that you have some prior knowledge or training, we do cover further education opportunities in Chapter 8).

1.1 US CYBERSECURITY JOB TITLES

We also assume that your first cybersecurity-related employment milestone will be to become a penetration tester or ethical hacker. Although these two job titles are probably the most popular, we should take a step back and appreciate that when you hear the term "cybersecurity professional" we could be referring to any one of the following job titles:

---

[1] ISC2 2015 Workforce Study

Cryptographer
- Source Code Auditor
- Digital Forensics Expert
- Forensic Analyst
- Incident Responder
- Security Architect
- Malware Analyst
- Network Security Engineer
- Security Analyst
- Computer Crime Investigator
- Chief Information Security Officer (CISO)
- Information Security Officer (ISO) or Director of Security
- Security Operations Center Analyst
- Prosecutor Specializing in Information Security Crime
- Technical Director and Deputy CISO
- Intrusion Analyst
- Vulnerability Researcher/Exploit Developer
- Security Auditor
- Disaster Recovery/Business Continuity Analyst/Manager

1.2 GENERAL "HACKER" CLASSIFICATIONS

Let us define the main categories of security professionals that will be referred to in this book. Professional hackers (or "crackers") will fit into one or several of the following categories:

1.2.1 White Hat Hacker

A "white hat hacker," (that is the category that we belong to if we aim to initially become a "penetration tester") will have permission to break security for nonmalicious reasons with the objective of patching or fixing-identified vulnerabilities.

1.2.2 Black Hat Hacker

On the complete opposite end of the scale is the "black hat cracker." Typically, a black hat hacker will try to break into a secure network to destroy data or make the network unusable.

1.2.3 Gray Hat Hacker

A "gray hat hacker" is a combination of a black and white hat. A gray hat hacker may surf the internet and hack into a computer system for the sole purpose of notifying the administrator that their system has a security defect. They may then offer to correct the defect for a fee. Many websites such as Facebook and Ebay offer bug bounties (please refer to Chapter 3 for more information), which means that anyone who finds a vulnerability or weakness can disclose the hole and receive a reward.

1.2.4 Blue Hat Hacker

A "blue hat hacker" (similar to gray hat) is someone who bug-tests a system or application prior to its launch, looking for exploits to be closed. It is worth mentioning that Microsoft uses the term "blue hat" to represent a series of security briefing events.

1.2.5 Blue and Red Teams

Another category that is relevant is "blue and red teams." In short: a red team attacks a network or computer system, and an opposing group – the blue team – defends it.

1.3 THE CONCEPT OF "BEING BAD TO BE GOOD"

One of the central facets of working within the cybersecurity industry is that you must "be bad to be good" or, said another way, "think like a hacker."

If you are confused by this statement, then consider the role of a professional combat soldier. A professional soldier is not inherently a bad person – quite the contrary: They are required to fight against an enemy that will have every intention of harming them with whatever weapons they have at their disposal. The combat soldier, therefore, needs effective weaponry and training – so the same applies to cyber-security professionals.

Cyber criminals are often highly skilled, resourceful, and deploy constantly evolving threats and attacks, are well equipped and knowl-edgeable and so must you be when you set yourself the goal of becoming a security professional – you must learn the dark-side skills to be able to defend against them.

1.4 KEY PENETRATION TESTER "KNOWLEDGE, SKILLS, AND ABILITIES" (KSA's)

The National Initiative for Cybersecurity Education[2] (NICE) developed the National Cybersecurity Workforce Framework[3] (the Workforce Framework) to define the cybersecurity workforce and provide a common taxonomy and lexicon by which to classify and categorize workers.

The Workforce Framework lists and defines 32 specialty areas of cybersecurity work and provides a description of each. It also identifies common tasks and knowledge, skills, and abilities (KSA's) associated with each specialty area. With this in mind, penetration testers fall within the "vulnerability assessment and management" specialty area which contains the following expected KSA's:

---

[2] http://csrc.nist.gov/nice/

[3] http://niccs.us-cert.gov/training/national-cybersecurity-workforce-framework

Knowledge of:

- Application vulnerabilities
- Content development
- Data backup, types of backups (e.g., full, incremental), and recovery concepts, and tools
- Different classes of attacks (e.g., passive, active, insider, close-in, distribution, etc.)
- Different operational-threat environments (e.g., first generation (script kiddies), second generation (non-nation state sponsored), and third generation (nation state sponsored))
- General attack stages (e.g., footprinting and scanning, enumeration, gaining access, escalation of privileges, maintaining access, network exploitation, covering tracks, etc.)
- Traffic flows across the network (e.g., Transmission Control Protocol (TCP) and Internet Protocol (IP), Open System Interconnection Model (OSI), Information Technology Infrastructure Library, v3 (ITIL))
- IA principles and organizational requirements (relevant to confidentiality, integrity, availability, authentication, nonrepudiation)
- Interpreted and compiled computer languages
- Local specialized system requirements (e.g., critical infrastructure systems that may not be used standard IT) for safety, performance, and reliability
- Network access, identity, and access management (e.g., public key infrastructure, PKI)
- Network protocols such as TCP/IP, Dynamic Host Configuration, Domain Name System (DNS), and directory services
- Network security architecture concepts including topology, protocols, components, and principles (e.g., application of defense-in-depth)
- Penetration testing principles, tools, and techniques (e.g., metasploit, neosploit, etc.)
- Programming language structures and logic
- Relevant laws, policies, procedures, or governance as they relate to work that may impact critical infrastructure
- System and application security threats and vulnerabilities

- System and application security threats and vulnerabilities (e.g., buffer overflow, mobile code, cross-site scripting, PL/SQL and injections, race conditions, covert channel, replay, return-oriented attacks, and malicious code)
- Systems diagnostic tools and fault identification techniques
- What constitutes a network attack and the relationship to both threats and vulnerabilities

Skills in:

- Applying host/network access controls (e.g., access control list)
- Assessing the robustness of security systems and designs
- Conducting vulnerability scans and recognizing vulnerabilities in security systems
- Detecting host- and network-based intrusions via intrusion detection technologies (e.g., Snort)
- Evaluating the trustworthiness of the supplier and/or product
- Mimicking threat behaviors
- Performing damage assessments
- Performing packet-level analysis (e.g., Wireshark, tcpdump, etc.)
- The use of penetration testing tools and techniques
- The use of social engineering techniques
- Using network analysis tools to identify vulnerabilities

Ability to:
- Identify systemic security issues on the basis of the analysis of vulnerability and configuration data

CHAPTER 2

The US Cybersecurity Industry

2.1 CURRENT AND EXPECTED GROWTH OF THE CYBERSECURITY INDUSTRY

If you were on the fence about joining the cybersecurity workforce, then this chapter will sway your decision! We will showcase four specific drivers fuelling the sectors growth. Simply put, cybersecurity incidents keep rising, and with this reality, so does IT-security spending. For example, small-and-medium-enterprise (SME) cyber budgets, on average, have increased by 51%[1] since 2012 (in tandem with an increase in cybersecurity recruitment spending).

2.1.1 Worldwide Cybersecurity Spending

Worldwide spending is expected to reach $71.1 billion in 2014, an increase of 7.9% over 2013, with the data-loss prevention segment recording the

---

[1] Global State of Information Security Survey 2014 (PwC)

fastest growth at 18.9%. Total information security spending will grow a further 8.2% in 2015 to reach $76.9 billion[2].

With a cumulative market value of $65.5 billion (2015–2020), the US Federal Cybersecurity market will grow steadily at about 6.2% compound annual growth rate (CAGR) while the private sector looks even more promising, growing from a current (2014) level of $95.6 billion to $155.74 billion by 2019, at a CAGR of 10.3%.

If you are serious about pursuing a career in Cybersecurity, here are four encouraging growth drivers to consider.

2.1.2 Growth Driver 1: Cybercrime
Cybercrime is big business and has finally reached the tipping point where consumers and regulators are demanding that businesses deploy effective solutions. McAfee estimates that the likely annual cost to the global economy from cyber crime is more than $400 billion.[3]

2.1.3 Growth Driver 2: The Internet-of-Things (IoT)
Cisco's Internet Business Solutions Group (IBSG) predicts some 25 billion devices will be connected by 2015, and 50 billion by 2020,[4] This eye-popping statistic is of concern from a privacy and security perspective, and vendors need experts to firm up their devices and IoT networks.

2.1.4 Growth Driver 3: Cybersecurity is Now a Main Street Issue
Everyone is now affected. Retail and healthcare-related attacks are reported on a daily basis, and have affected tens of millions of consumers that has prompted mainstream awareness to the problem.

2.1.5 Growth Driver 4: Regulatory Compliance
Regulatory compliance has been a major factor driving spending on security. Key government agencies to study include: The Federal Financial

---

[2] Global State of Information Security Survey 2014 (PwC)
[3] Net Losses: Estimating the Global Cost of Cybercrime Economic Impact of Cybercrime, June, 2014
[4] "The Internet of Things," Cisco Internet Business Solutions Group, http://share.cisco.com/internet-of-things.html

Institutions Examination Council (FFIEC) and The Federal Energy Regulatory Commission (FERC) and you should also review: The Health Insurance Portability and Accountability Act (HIPAA); Family Educational Rights and Privacy Act (FERPA); Federal Information Security Management Act (FISMA) and Federal Energy Regulatory Commission (FERC).

2.2 EMPLOYMENT OPPORTUNITIES

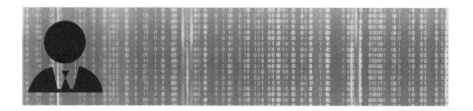

The cybersecurity market-growth potential is enormous. In parallel with this surge, is the demand for cybersecurity job seekers.

2.2.1 Private Sector Demand
Demand for cybersecurity professionals grew 3.5 times faster over the past 5 years than demand for other IT jobs in general, and about 12 times faster than for all jobs. In fact, CareerBuilder,[5] an online employment website with more than 300,000 employers stated that demand for information security professionals is projected to grow 22% from 2010 to 2020.

2.2.2 Public Sector Demand
According to former Defense Secretary Robert Gates[6], the Pentagon is "desperately short of people who have capabilities (defensive and offensive cybersecurity war skills) in all the services." As a response to the lack of qualified and skilled cyber professionals, the US Government launched the National Initiative for Cybersecurity Careers and Studies[7] (NICCS) to

---

[5] Source: Based on the National Association of Colleges and Employers report The Job Outlook for the Class of 2014
[6] Cyber In Security Strengthening the Federal Cybersecurity Workforce, conducted by Partnership for Public Service and Booz Allen Hamilton, July 2009.
[7] http://niccs.us-cert.gov/

develop a technologically skilled workforce. Indeed, as we shall discover in Chapter 6, the US Government has created an "Internship Program," managed by the Office of Personnel Management that offers students and recent graduates various opportunities to engage in experiential education.

2.3 2015 SALARY GUIDE FOR CYBERSECURITY PROFESSIONALS

Predicated salaries for cybersecurity professionals in 2015[8] is promising. Here are some examples:

Security IT Professionals	Salaries in 2014 ($)	Salaries in 2015 ($)	Change (%)
Data security analyst	$100,500–137,250	$106,250–149,000	7.4
Systems security administrator	$95,250–131,500	$100,000–140,250	6.0
Network security administrator	$95,000–130,750	$99,250–138,500	5.3
Network security engineer	$99,750–131,250	$105,000–141,500	6.7
Information systems security manager	$115,250–160,000	$122,250–171,250	6.6

To further compound this growth, according to the U.S. Bureau of Labor Statistics[9] in 2015, IT-security specialist employment will explode by 37% from 2012 to 2022, over 3 times faster than the 11% average for

[8] 2015 Salary Guide For Technology Professionals – Robert Half Technology
[9] U.S. Bureau of Labor Statistics – Occupational Handbook 2015

all occupations, placing it among the nation's fastest growing employment fields within the nation.

2.4 ENTRY-LEVEL POSITIONS

It is unusual to start your career as an information security professional, rather, it is more of a role that you will most likely move into. With this in mind, typical entry-level job titles include: help desk technician; IT support technician/desktop support; IT support engineer; Microsoft Windows IT support technician; Microsoft Windows level-1 support engineer; IT infrastructure support consultant; SQL IT application support analyst; database administrator (including Oracle DBA); enterprise resource planning; Linux administrator and system administrator.

CHAPTER 3

17 Tips on How to Land Your First Cybersecurity Job

Let us first establish whether or not you have the right temperament to perform well in a penetration-testing role, and then, let us take a look at 17 tips to help you hone your skills and employability.

3.1 TIP 1: DEVELOP THE RIGHT ATTITUDE

It is unlikely that you will be a competent penetration tester if you are not passionate about IT security and technology. Owing to the relentless onslaught of attack and identification of new attack vectors, a penetration tester has to constantly learn new tools, processes, and methodologies.

3.2 TIP 2: CURIOSITY IS KEY

You purchased this book because you are, at the very least, curious about finding a cybersecurity-related job. Hackers are, by their nature, curious people, but why is curiosity important for someone interested in starting a career in cybersecurity?

Consider the following four reasons:

Being curious makes your mind active instead of passive! Curious people ask questions and search for answers. A hacker's mind is always active. Think of your mind as a muscle that becomes stronger through constant exercise and mental stimulation. Set yourself the goal of continuously learning about cybersecurity and you will make your mind stronger.

Curiosity trains your mind to be more observant to new concepts! Being curious about technologies that interest you will make your mind expect and anticipate new concepts. When new concepts and ideas arise, you will be better placed to understand them. Just think how many great ideas and security preventions have been lost through a lack of curiosity.

Open up new worlds and possibilities! By being curious you will see new possibilities that are normally invisible to the average end user. They are hidden behind the surface of normal life, and it takes a curious mind to find them.

Curiosity brings excitement to your life! The life of curious people (Hackers!) is far from boring and certainly never routine. There are always new challenges and opportunities that attract their attention, and there are always new cybersecurity "toys" to play with.

3.3 TIP 3: DEVELOP TECHNICAL PROWESS

Penetration testing is an extremely technical discipline. You must be able to understand not only how technologies work at a low level but you must also be able to subvert controls in a repeatable and methodical way, and learn constantly as new software and hardware updates are released.

3.4 TIP 4: GET INVOLVED IN YOUR LOCAL COMMUNITY

Needless to say, getting involved with hacker groups or Linux user clubs in your local town or city is a great way to start laying the foundations of your cybersecurity career. Meetup.com for example is a great resource. We counted 250 hacker groups with 45,000 members in the United States alone. Not only will it be fun to meet like-minded people but joining the group will also facilitate networking opportunities. At the very least, you stand to make new friends who will offer you free advice on how to break into the industry. Volunteer to present a tutorial or specific piece of research at your club. That is a great way to force yourself to become an "expert" within a particular technology.

Look to see if there are any BSides[1] events near you. BSides is an excellent organization that has chapters in every major city in the United States. BSides has come to be known as a "conference by the community for the community" and events are generally free to attend.

3.5 TIP 5: TAKE PART IN COMPETITIONS

Extending from Tip 4, you might likely discover that your local hacking club or group submits teams for competitions. Competitions like

---

[1] http://www.securitybsides.com/w/page/12194156/FrontPage

"capture the flag (CTF)" are an excellent way to improve your penetration skills, social communicative skills, and of course, to network. Incidentally, it is also very common for recruitment agents to be present at CTF events. Here is a list of resources to get you started:

CTF Time (https://ctftime.org/event/list/)
List of cyber competitions in the USA (http://niccs.us-cert.gov/education/cyber-competitions-repository)
Another excellent list of competitions (http://ctf.forgottensec.com/wiki/index.php?title=Main_Page)
Cyber attack and defense training range (http://threatspace.net/)
Capture the flag puzzles (https://sb2.threatspace.net/)
Fall National Cyber League Competition (http://www.nationalcyberleague.org/registration.shtml)
National Collegiate Cyber Defense Competition (http://www.nationalccdc.org/)

3.6 TIP 6: JOIN NEWSLETTERS AND READ BLOGS

Email lists have been around since the early days of the Internet but they are still an excellent way to stay abreast of what is happening in cybersecurity. Here are some newsletters that you should consider signing up to.

SecureRoot (http://secureroot.com/): It was created in the 1990s and quickly grew with its simple to use and friendly interface.
SecList (http://seclists.org/): SecList provides web archives and RSS feeds (now including message extracts).

SecurityFocus (http://www.securityfocus.com/): SecurityFocus has been a mainstay in the security community. It contains original news content about detailed technical papers and guest columnists.

BugTraq (http://www.securityfocus.com/archive/1): BugTraq is a high-volume, full-disclosure mailing list for the detailed discussion and announcement of computer security vulnerabilities.

United States Computer Emergency Readiness Team (US-CERT) (https://www.us-cert.gov/mailing-lists-and-feeds): The US-CERT offers mailing lists and feeds for a variety of products including the National Cyber Awareness System and Current Activity updates.

oss-security Mailing List Charter (http://oss-security.openwall.org/wiki/mailing-lists/oss-security): The open-source security (oss-security) group encourages public discussion of security flaws, concepts, and practices in the open-source community. The members of this group include, but are not limited to, open-source projects, distributors, researchers, and developers.

Handler's Diary (https://isc.sans.edu//diary.html): The Handler's Diary is more of a blog than a mailing list, but it is just as important nonetheless. It is written by various volunteers, and published by SANS.

SANS: Cybersecurity Newsletters (http://www.sans.org/newsletters/): SANS NewsBites is a semiweekly high-level executive summary of the most important news articles that have been published on computer security.

Microsoft Security Newsletter (http://technet.microsoft.com/en-us/security/dd162324.aspx): This newsletter will help you stay up to date with security insights, resources, best practices, and events for IT professionals and developers.

CSO Security and Risk Newsletters (http://www.csoonline.com/newsletters): CSO provides news, analysis and research on a broad range of security and risk topics – all taken from a management perspective.

Security News and Articles (http://nakedsecurity.sophos.com/): This award-winning news, opinion, advice, and research newsletter has a wide range of articles and is certainly recommended as a good source of information.

3.7 TIP 7: MASTER POPULAR HACKING TOOLS

As we established in Tips 1, 2, and 3 – education and self-learning are vital components to becoming a penetration tester. There are plenty of inexpensive or free online resources to gain basic knowledge around testing and using the tools. Your mastery of these hacking tools will move you up to a level whereby you can hold a competent conversation in an interview, or demonstrate working knowledge of, for example, Metasploit or Burp Suite. Great resources for mastering popular hacking tools can be found on sites like Concise-Courses.com SecurityTube, Udemy, OWASP, and YouTube.

3.8 TIP 8: BECOME A KALI LINUX POWER USER

This is an extension of Tip 7, BackTrack was the Linux Pentesting Distro of choice until the developers decided that it was time to relaunch a new distro: Kali Linux. At the last count, there were over 250 penetration-testing tools contained within Kali Linux.

We highly recommended that your Kali Linux installation is hard booted, rather than using a Virtual Machine. In our experience, Wireless Cards such as the Alpha AWU do not work as well when they bridge over the virtualized partition; restrictions which could impact your ability to master some tools (see Tip #7).

3.9 TIP 9: CREATE A HOME LAB

You should already be familiar with the fundamentals of computing, but if you have not done so already, setup a home network or better still, a lab, or as some call it, a "rig." Installing DVWA (Damn Vulnerable Web App) is an excellent PHP/MySQL insecure web application that you can use to test your skills.

Many IT-security companies and even individual penetration testers or network/systems technicians will create their own labs where they configure and reconfigure systems, try out exploits, compromise the security of computers, and then try and harden defenses and attack them.

This might sound expensive but you can build a lab up over time if you have the resources (and space). Various Internet auction sites and local recycling groups are a great source of inexpensive hardware. Linux favors that run on lower-specification systems can be found and virtualisation can also enable you to run several virtual servers on a single physical host (and to recover them easily if you end up breaking the operating system).

3.10 TIP 10: BECOME A CODE MONKEY

0 1 0 1
1 0 1 1
0 1 1 0

The ability to write code or program is always an advantage and it certainly will help you understand web applications. It is not absolutely vital, but learning one or more languages will help. The C programming language has a lot of use within application security, but Java, Python, or Ruby will do just fine.

3.11 TIP 11: FIND BUGS!

Bug bounties are an excellent way to prove your skills and prowess with sites such as "Bugcrowd" paying sizeable amounts to their best bug hunters. Finding and documenting how you found a bug and placing this on your resume will certainly raise heads in the HR/Recruitment Office so sign up to at least one bug bounty site today!

3.12 TIP 12: PARTICIPATE IN OPEN-SOURCE PROJECTS

Stemming on the back of learning how to code is our recommendation to participate on an open-source project. Find a subject or project that you are interested in on Github and get involved! The organizer of the project will almost certainly be grateful for the extra help, and may even be willing to provide a testimonial on the work you submitted (which you can place on your LinkedIn profile).

Furthermore, participating in an open-source project will allow you to differentiate yourself from your peers by acquiring a niche skill. For example, why not find a mobile/cell-phone hacking project – this is a growth area and would further your employment marketability.

3.13 TIP 13: BRUSH UP ON YOUR WRITTEN SKILLS

Written skills are vital when applying for a cybersecurity job. Being able to effectively communicate in lay terms is what can separate a serious professional from a script kiddie. If you want to excel at working in cybersecurity, then learn how to write effective audits and reports that detail your penetration test or forensic analysis.

3.14 TIP 14: ATTEND CYBERSECURITY CONFERENCES AND VOLUNTEER

Attending conferences is obviously a fantastic way to network, learn about new technologies and research, and seek opportunities! Although ticket prices can be expensive, think about presenting at a conference. Cybersecurity conferences always need speakers, which they generate through a process known as "call for papers." Simply submit your research/presentation proposal and wait to see if they accept it. Having your resume mention that you spoke at a conference is a sure-fire way to alert the interest of a recruiter.

Remember, that you can also volunteer at conferences! Volunteering is a great way to impress enthusiasm on your resume and is again an excellent networking opportunity since you will be working with the event organizers who most likely work within the cybersecurity industry. DEF CON is one of the largest conferences on the West Coast, and Shmoocon is a popular conference on the East Coast. Smaller conferences include: Hacktivity, ToorCon, HackFest, and Hacker Halted. For a comprehensive list of cybersecurity conferences visit: http://www.concise-courses.com/security/conferences-of-2015/

3.15 TIP 15: LEARN LINUX!

This is essentially an extension of Tip 8 but nonetheless, understanding Linux will help your career. Nearly all useful hacking tools are developed specifically for Linux, so by extension, understanding shortcut commands and so forth will increase your efficiency and effectiveness.

3.16 TIP 16: GET WORK EXPERIENCE

OK! Likely you are thinking that everything so far is all well and good – but the truth still remains – when applying for a security role you will be asked for experience, or better said, your employer will check your resume to see what kind of experience you have, before inviting you to the next stage.

CHAPTER 4

Networking Advice for Cybersecurity Job Seekers

4.1 USING LinkedIn TO SECURE A CYBERSECURITY JOB

As an information security professional, networking will be the single most powerful marketing tactic you will have to start, accelerate, and sustain your career in cybersecurity. Relationships are the catalyst for success because, said simply, people do business with those they like and trust. There is no getting around it but LinkedIn is huge and you absolutely *must* have a profile.

Here is a quick tip to assist you on your quest to securing employment in the cybersecurity space: Find organizations that you would like to work for and identify individuals currently employed in the role you are seeking.

Further, identify which LinkedIn groups they are members of and join one of those groups, preferably one that has a large subscription base and has been deemed by LinkedIn to be "very active."

Now, as you probably know, you need to have a LinkedIn member's email address before being allowed to contact them directly. However, when you both share the same group, you can contact that person directly (i.e., no email is required). To find that individual and connect with them, click on "Interests > Groups" from the dropdown on your LinkedIn navigation (see the drop-down menu in the image below).

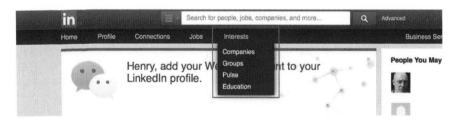

The next page will show the groups to which you belong. Click the group that your target is also a member of and you will be taken to the Groups' dashboard.

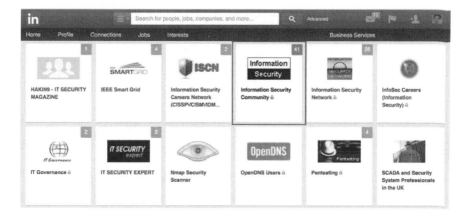

Click on the "Members" tab (see the image below) and type in the targets name and, if he or she is in the same group as you are in, you will have an opportunity to message them directly.

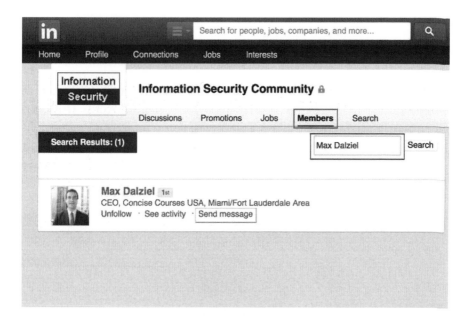

When you contact them, ask for advice regarding how they developed their career. In our experience, professionals enjoy giving advice and you will likely be surprised by the positive replies and assistance you receive.

Please make sure that your first message is *not* to directly ask for a job because people are unlikely to respond. Another more obvious method to network is to interact within LinkedIn group discussions. Using the keywords "information security" we discovered 2,858 possible LinkedIn groups to join! From this huge list, select a dozen groups that you feel you can contribute and participate in, and become an active member of. If you are an active member of the niche community, you will rapidly become accepted and therefore be respected when you reach out to professionals of interest with regards to your job search.

If you wish to take this to the highest level, you can request an "informational interview" when you initiate contact. We will cover this in Chapter 7, specifically in Section 7.3 where you ask your target questions about their path to securing employment and pick their brains for advice, tips, and of course, contacts and referrals! If you need inspiration for companies you would like to work for, please refer to Section 6.1, which contains a list of organizations that either offer internships or graduate positions).

4.2 HOW TO IDENTIFY INFLUENCERS

As mentioned in the previous section, your goal as a job seeker is to create friendships with a view to getting recognized and considered for positions when they become available.

But how do you do this? We will look at the more obvious methods shortly but here is a tip to find influential cybersecurity professionals that you can network with: look at speaker lists on past and upcoming security conferences and events. For a comprehensive list refer to: http://www.concise-courses.com/security/conferences-of-2015/ for cyber events in 2015. Look at the names and subjects of the speakers (their bio's often mention their organization) and see who interests you! Contact them through LinkedIn (or by email or Twitter), and let them know how much you enjoyed their presentation and research. You can even send them a link to similar research or something that adds value to their work. The point is this: Everyone loves flattery, and this will initiate a conversation with a view to asking for their advice. A variation of the above is to search through SlideShare for presentations using keywords like "penetration testing," "Hacking," "BYOD," or any other similar key phrases. More often than not you will discover presentations including contact details of the author and apply the same principles.

4.3 WHAT NOT TO DO ON LinkedIn

We have mostly focused on LinkedIn for good reason. It is the most valued of all professional networks. Here are some tips from a cybersecurity's point of view to avoid when using LinkedIn:

- Hackers have a reputation of being shy and introverted. Be the opposite and have a professional photo. Not having a photo might lead to lost connections.
- Make sure your photo is of you, that is, no dog, baby, hacker logo, and so forth, just keep it 100% professional.
- Make sure your photo is recent (if you have an interview and look older in person, then the interviewer will be distracted by your appearance).
- Make sure you only update your status with professional information, new penetration skills you have learned, for example, nothing personal or social should be in your profile.
- Always write in the first person to add energy and personality. Remember that penetration testers need good grammar and writing skills (since you will be writing reports) so make sure your English is faultless.
- List all your past jobs and volunteering because you never know what employers are seeking (TIP! there are volunteering opportunities for DEF CON and most InfoSec Conferences, see Tip 14)
- Lastly, do not forget to tweak your privacy settings to prevent your employer snooping!

4.4 USING TWITTER TO SECURE A CYBERSECURITY JOB

Given the speed and consistency with which vulnerabilities are discovered, and the time-sensitive nature with which they need to be handled, Twitter is without a doubt the most popular social media platform for cybersecurity professionals. Use the steps outlined previously to find out if your targets have a Twitter handle. Follow them and retweet, favorite, or mention their tweets. The goal here is to get noticed and start communicating. Here is our list of recommended cybersecurity professionals to follow:

Max Dalziel: @conciseonline shares free cybersecurity courses, news and invitations to his live web show "Hacker Hotshots".

Mikko Hypponen: @mikko has received many accolades, among them being voted one of the 50 most important people on the web by PC world magazine. As a keynote speaker, he has spoken for TED and Google. His tweets are wide ranging and occasionally technical. He shares lots of articles from the F-secure blog, where he has worked since 1999.

Jack Daniel: @jack_daniel is co-founder of Security BSides and he tweets his thoughts on information security as well as insightful quotes.

Bruce Schneier: @schneierblog is an internationally recognized security guru and author of 12 books on security. He primarily tweets about tech and surveillance.

Josh Corman: @joshcorman is the CTO for Sonatype, having previously been a security researcher and strategist at Akamai Technologies. He tweets about cybersecurity and DevOps.

Richard Stiennon: @stiennon is a security industry analyst reporting on cyber defense, he is also the author of Surviving Cyberwar.

@stiennon is very active on both Twitter accounts, tweeting about surveillance, cybersecurity, and cyberwar.

Kevin Mitnick: @kevinmitnick is an American computer security consultant, author and hacker (one of the first internationally known). He is currently the founder and owner of Mitnick Security Consulting.

Richard Bejtlich: @taosecurity has been stopping digital intruders since 1998. Richard is currently chief security strategist at FireEye, and he tweets about tech, cybersecurity, and information security

Chris Hadnagy: @humanhacker is a speaker, teacher, and recognized security expert. He has spent the last 16 years in security and technology, specializing in understanding the ways in which malicious attackers are able to exploit human weaknesses to obtain access to information and resources.

Danny Yadron: @dannyyadron is the Wall Street Journal's cybersecurity reporter. Danny shares lots of the articles he publishes in the WSJ, other publishers' articles on security issues and mixes in a good dose of humor to keep things interesting.

CHAPTER 5

How to Create a Cybersecurity Resume

5.1 RESUME ADVICE

Aside from the basics listed below, let us take a look at what an ideal resume should look like for somebody looking to pursue a career in cybersecurity:

5.1.1 The Basics

- Presentation (must be white paper)
- Remember to place important details on the "Hot Spot" (top left section)
- Do not exceed two pages of 8.5×11

5.1.2 Making the Most of Your Skills

Your knowledge, skills, and abilities (KSA's) of specific protocols and technologies must be made prominent since they will clarify your suitability for the role.

5.1.3 Making the Most of Your Interests

Refer back to Chapter 3 and specifically Tip 4, Tip 5, Tip 9, and Tip 15 since these will all add personality and color to your resume.

5.1.4 Keep Your Resume Updated

It is crucial to demonstrate that you are constantly learning new skills, processes, and tools.

5.2 CYBERSECURITY RESUME

A cybersecurity resume needs several items to be included. In the image below notice how this sample resume has included references to Github and StackOverFlow – two community-driven tech sites that instantly demonstrate your tech prowess and involvement in the sector.

Harry Hacker

Penetration Tester

Tel: +1 212 345 5566
Site: hacker.com
StackOverflow: stackoverflow/user/

Email: hh@hacker.com
Twitter: @conciseonline
GitHub: github.com/

From an early age I have been using Linux and during my secondary school I became interested in the information security arena doing anything from computer/network auditing, to vulnerability assessments and penetration testing.

Education, Training & Certifications

Certified Ethical Hacker
2014–2014   Professional Penetration Testing Certification

Cyber Security Major
2012–2014   University of Southern California

Relevant Courses:
- Security technologies and enforcement
- System management
- Statistical analysis of cyber attacks
- Web technologies
- Advanced protocols

As mentioned, it would also be a good idea to list all of your cybersecurity-related skills. A cybersecurity HR or hiring manager will likely be recruiting individuals with specific penetration skills – so it is vital that you include your as many as skills as possible.

Cyber Security Major

2012–2014   University of Southern California

Relevant Courses:
- Security technologies and enforcement
- System management
- Statistical analysis of cyber attacks
- Web technologies
- Advanced protocols

Skills

- Network Engineering
- Penetration Testing
- SEO Algorithms
- Software Engineering
- Python,PHP, JavaScript, C(++), Delphi, *SQL, and LaTeX
- Microsoft's MVC Web Framework. • SEO Algorithms
- Software Engineering
- Objective-C

Experience

20014–2014   **Security Research and Development Intern, Summer 2014**
Concise Courses InfoSecurity

I worked with the Concise Courses Team, where I was given the task of taking a new security product from the beta stage to its' successful launch. During my time at Concise Courses I also contributed in a penetration test against a client's iOS and Android application, identifying vulnerabilities and testing the client's fixes in a submitted code review. In addition, I analysed a piece of malware to establish how it worked and suggested possible fixes.

Of significant value was the experience I gained in understanding some of the current Advanced Persistent Threats to businesses and different methods of attack, such as SQL Injection and XSS Cross Site Scripting as common in the OWASP Top Ten.

The image below illustrates further information that we feel is necessary to include in your resume for first-time job seekers. Including information like your attendance and participation (even as a volunteer) at cybersecurity conferences, your interests and professional membership affiliations will all help with your application.

Cyber Security Events And Conference Attendance

Over the past 5 years I have made an effort to attend many cyber security events around the industry to build contacts, learn new skills, and gain critical feedback on my ideas and research. Events I have been to include Toorcon, Hacker Halted, BlackHat, Suits and Spookes, Nullcon and RSA San Francisco.

Open Source Projects

BitLithium.net (a smart script that extracts intelligence from the Bitcoin network), AndroidSMSExport.com (a web and desktop application that can convert Android text messages to CSV, HTML or PDF) TriStateMe.net (a web application to perform direct and reverse Tri State Area phone numbers lookups the results are exported).

Professional Memberships

- ISACA
- EC Council (Certified Ethical Hacker)
- CompTIA
- ISC2

Hobbies and Interests

I am interested in anything and everything to do with Information Security. I started a local hacking Meetup Group in downtown New York which attracts 40+ hackers on the first friday of the month. The goal of the group is to creates opportunities for individuals to both present and participate in an intimate atmosphere that encourages collaboration. It is an intense event with discussions, demos, and more!

5.2.1 Federal Internship Resume Tips

If you are applying for a federal position then your resume needs to have the following additions (these next two points only apply to those candidates that have already worked for the federal government):

- You must include your "general schedule" information (this is with reference to your pay scale and structure).

- Number of hours worked per week in previous positions for the government.

If you are applying for a federal internship for the *first time* then you must mention the following information:

- The full title of the department you are seeking employment or an internship with, that is, do not write three letter abbreviations like FBI; write the full name of the agency.
- Federal resumes require that you include the amount of semester hours your course took (major, etc.)

CHAPTER 6

Cybersecurity Job Resources

6.1 SHOULD YOU DO AN UNPAID INTERNSHIP?

Of course, a paid position is better, but if you lack the experience, or do not have a computer science major (or equivalent) then often an unpaid internship will produce significant long-term benefits.

Here is a quick statistic that will likely influence your motivation to secure a paid or unpaid internship: 75% of employers prefer new graduates with work experience[1]!

In the next section, we will look at various private and public opportunities available to you, but let us just establish the benefits of an unpaid internship:

Benefit 1: Gain valuable knowledge, skills, and abilities (KSAs): An internship provides the opportunity to gain "hands-on" work experience and skills that are essential in your cybersecurity career.

Benefit 2: Gain an edge in the job market: Although there is huge demand for cybersecurity professionals, the demand is mostly for *experienced* professionals, And an internship is often the best way to show that experience.

Benefit 3: Potential Transition Into Full Time Employment: It is a simple but true fact that employers see interns as prospective employees and many finish their internships and continue working with the company full time.

---

[1] Source: National Association of Colleges and Employers report, The Job Outlook for the Class of 2014

6.2 US FEDERAL INTERNSHIPS AND GRADUATE OPPORTUNITIES

To address a shortage of skilled graduate labor in the United States, especially cyber experts, President Obama signed Executive Order 13562, entitled "Recruiting and Hiring Students and Recent Graduates," on December 27, 2010.

This Executive Order established the "Internship Program" for current students and the "Recent Graduates Program" for people who have recently graduated from qualifying educational institutions or programs (2 years from the date the graduate completed an academic course of study).

Many of these federal internship opportunities can open the door to full-time jobs and serve as an excellent way of entering the federal workforce. Several federal internships are within the intelligence community (IC) agencies. The IC is committed to growing the next generation of intelligence professionals (especially cyber professionals) by offering current students a variety of temporary employment and scholarship opportunities (for a list of IC agencies please refer to the end of this section).

Types of Internships and Opportunities

Managed by the Office of Personnel Management, there are three pathways:

> *The Internship Program*: This program provides enrolled students exposure to the Federal Government (see our list for examples and opportunities).
> *The Recent Graduate Program*: This program is designed for new graduates and those who graduated in the past 2 years. This program provides developmental opportunities and training.

The Presidential Management Fellows Program: This program, also known as the PMF, is a leadership-development program for entry-level advanced degree candidates.

Let us now take a look at existing opportunities within these programs.

Government Internship Opportunities with the Federal Government Intelligence Agencies

- *Agency*: Central Intelligence Agency
  - *Program*: CIA Student Work Program
  - *Link*: https://www.cia.gov/careers/student-opportunities/index.html
  - *Description*: Work and shadow IT security professionals in the CIA
- *Agency*: Department of Energy, Office of Intelligence and Counterintelligence
  - *Program*: The "DOE Scholars Program"
  - *Link*: https://www.cia.gov/careers/student-opportunities/index.html
  - *Description*: The DOE Scholars Program introduces students or recent college graduates to DOE's mission and operations.
- *Agency*: Department of Homeland Security, Intelligence and Analysis
  - *Program*: Secretary's Honors Program
  - *Link*: http://www.dhs.gov/secretarys-honors-program
  - *Description*: A recruitment initiative for exceptional recent graduates.
- *Agency*: Department of Homeland Security, Intelligence and Analysis
  - *Program*: SHP Cyber Student Volunteer Initiative
  - *Link*: http://www.dhs.gov/secretarys-honors-program
  - *Description*: This program is for 100 unpaid student volunteers with assignments available in over 60 locations across the country, participating in, for example, U.S. Immigration and Customs Enforcement, computer forensics, the U.S. Secret Service and the U.S. Coast Guard. Student volunteers in the program gain invaluable hands-on experience and exposure to the work done by DHS cybersecurity professionals, and perform a broad range of duties in support of DHS cybersecurity mission.

- *Agency*: Department of Homeland Security, Intelligence and Analysis
  - *Program*: Presidential Management Fellows Program
  - *Link*: http://www.dhs.gov/presidential-management-fellows-program
  - *Description*: This program is designed for graduate-level students to attract outstanding men and women from a variety of academic disciplines and career paths who have a clear interest in, and commitment to, excellence in the leadership and management of public policies and programs.
- *Agency*: Department of Homeland Security, Intelligence and Analysis
  - *Program*: Acquisition Professional Career Program
  - *Link*: http://www.dhs.gov/acquisition-professional-career-program
  - *Description*: Acquisition Professional Career Program participants work in one of six career fields, each of which plays a vital role in department acquisition (which includes systems security engineers).
- *Agency*: Department of State, Intelligence and Research
  - *Program*: Student Programs
  - *Link*: http://careers.state.gov/students/programs
  - *Description*: The U.S. Department of State offers two programs for high-school, undergraduate, graduate, and postgraduate students who are interested in working in a foreign affairs environment.
- *Agency*: Department of Treasury, Office of Intelligence and Analysis
  - *Program*: Pathways Program
  - *Link*: http://www.treasury.gov/careers/Pages/pathways-programs.aspx
  - *Description*: Pathways, short for the Pathways Program, are a new series of programs developed by the Office of Personnel Management (OPM) to reform the student hiring programs across the government. The Pathways Programs contains three main hiring options: Internship Program, Recent Graduate Program, and the Presidential Management Fellows (PMF) Program (similar to the DHS above).
- *Agency*: Defense Intelligence Agency
  - *Program*: Academic Semester Internship Program

- *Link*: http://www.dia.mil/careers/students/
- *Description*: Provides undergraduate seniors and graduate students enrolled as full-time degree seeking students the opportunity to gain practical work experience in intelligence analysis while enrolled in classes.
- *Agency*: Defense Intelligence Agency
  - *Program*: Cooperative Education Program
  - *Link*: http://www.dia.mil/careers/students/
  - *Description*: Provides a select number of talented undergraduate and graduate students the opportunity to gain valuable work experience in combination with their academic studies.
- *Agency*: Defense Intelligence Agency
  - *Program*: National Intelligence Scholars Program
  - *Link*: http://www.dia.mil/careers/students/
  - *Description*: Affords a small select number of college graduates the opportunity to obtain a quality education that will get their career off to a successful beginning.
- *Agency*: Drug Enforcement Administration
  - *Program*: Internship Program
  - *Link*: http://www.justice.gov/dea/careers/student-entry-level.shtml
  - *Description*: Shadow the activities of cyber and law professionals in the DEA.
- *Agency*: Federal Bureau of Investigation
  - *Program*: Honors Internship Program
  - *Link*: https://www.fbijobs.gov/231.asp
  - *Description*: Paid FBI Internship Opportunity in which you shadow and assist the activities of law enforcement.
- *Agency*: Federal Bureau of Investigation
  - *Program*: Volunteer Internship Program (unpaid):
  - *Link*: https://www.fbijobs.gov/239.asp
  - *Description*: The FBI Volunteer Internship Program is an unpaid internship opportunity that offers undergraduates (junior or senior), graduates or postdoctorate students throughout the country an exciting insider's view of FBI operations and an opportunity to explore career opportunities within the Bureau.
- *Agency*: Federal Bureau of Investigation
  - *Program*: Laboratory Division's Visiting Science Program
  - *Link*: https://www.fbijobs.gov/242.asp

- *Description*: Students, postgraduates, and faculty are eligible to apply for the FBI Visiting Scientist Program.
- *Agency*: National Geospatial Intelligence Agency
  - *Program*: NGA Student Employment Program
  - *Link*: https://www1.nga.mil/Careers/StudentOpp/Internships/Pages/default.aspx
  - *Description*: Applicants must be enrolled in an associate, baccalaureate, graduate, or postgraduate degree program with coursework related to NGA's mission.
- *Agency*: National Geospatial Intelligence Agency
  - *Program*: NGA Scholarship Programs & Stokes Scholarship Program
  - *Link*: https://www1.nga.mil/Careers/StudentOpp/Scholarships/Pages/default.aspx
  - *Description*: The NGA Stokes Scholarship Program is designed for high-achieving college undergraduates who have demonstrated financial need and interest in a career with NGA.
- *Agency*: National Security Agency
  - *Program*: NSA internships
  - *Link*: http://www.nsa.gov/careers/opportunities_4_u/students/index.shtml
  - *Description*: Co-op program, scholarships, and work–study programs will help you to develop and shape your career well before your studies are through.
- *Agency*: National Security Agency
  - *Program*: Undergraduate Positions
  - *Link*: http://www.nsa.gov/careers/opportunities_4_u/students/undergraduate/index.shtml
  - *Description*: As a college undergrad, you can gain the experience you need while working toward your degree.
- *Agency*: National Security Agency
  - *Program*: Graduate Positions
  - *Link*: http://www.nsa.gov/careers/opportunities_4_u/students/graduate/index.shtml
  - *Description*: If you are working toward your MS or PhD in a field critical to NSA's mission, they can help you gain the practical experience you need.

IC Agency Employment Websites

For other cybersecurity related employment opportunities within the US IC, please visit the following URL's for the latest information:

- CIA (Central Intelligence Agency) https://www.cia.gov/careers/index.html
- DEA (Drug Enforcement Agency) http://www.dea.gov/resources/job_applicants.html
- DHS (Department Homeland Security) http://www.dhs.gov/xabout/careers/
- DIA (Defense Intelligence Agency) http://www.dia.mil/careers.aspx
- DOE (Department of Energy) http://jobs.energy.gov/
- DoS (Department of State) http://www.state.gov/careers/
- FBI (Federal Bureau of Investigation) https://www.fbijobs.gov
- NGA (National Geospatial Agency) https://www1.nga.mil/Careers/Pages/default.aspx
- NRO (National Reconnaissance Office) http://www.nro.mil/careers/careers.html
- NSA (National Security Agency) http://www.nsa.gov/careers/
- ODNI (Director of National Intelligence) http://www.odni.gov
- Treasury (US Treasury) http://www.treasury.gov/organization/employment/
- US Army (US Army) http://www.cpol.army.mil/
- USAF (US Air Force) http://www.afciviliancareers.com/index.php
- USCG (US Coast Gaurd) http://www.uscg.mil/civilian/
- USMC (United States Marine Corps) http://www.quantico.marines.mil/UnitHome.aspx
- US Navy (US Army) http://www.navy.com/careers.html

6.3 THE FEDERAL HIRING PROCESS

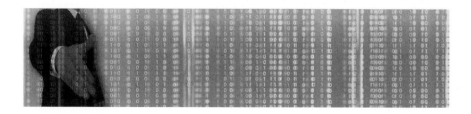

If you are not selected during any of the steps or process outlined don't get discouraged. Refine your resume and KSA's (knowledge, skills, and abilities), and continue to apply to relevant openings.

The Federal hiring process is a lot longer than in the private sector because of stricter processes in handling job applications. In addition, being able to apply for positions through the links listed previously, the main resource for your quest to seek Federal employment (or internship) is to use the US government's USAJobs.gov website. USAJobs.gov has inbuilt functionality that allows applicants to see how their applications are progressing through the organization's hiring processes.

6.4 US PRIVATE SECTOR INTERNSHIPS AND GRADUATE OPPORTUNITIES

These companies have recently attended cybersecurity job fairs at several universities throughout the United States to recruit students – making them some of the nation's most active recruiters:

- Booz Allen Hamilton
- Deloitte
- ExecuTech Strategic Consulting
- General Dynamics
- ManTech International
- MOSAIC Technologies Group
- Northrop Grumman
- Radius Technology Group
- Science Applications International Corporation (SAIC)
- The Boeing Company
- URS (United Research Services)
- Science Applications International Corporation
- PricewaterhouseCoopers
- Hewlett-Packard
- Dell
- CACI (Consolidated Analysis Center, Incorporated)
- Accenture

Here is our list of corporate internships opportunities in the United States:

Chevron IT Internship (http://careers.chevron.com/disciplines/index_of_disciplines/information_technology/it_internships.aspx)

Apple Internship (http://www.apple.com/jobs/us/students.html#internship)

GE General IT Internship (http://careers.gm.com/student-center.html)

GE General Specialized IT Internships (http://www.ge.com/careers/culture/university-students/information-technology-leadership-program/united-states)

Valero Energy Internships (http:://www.valero.com/Careers/UniversityRecruiting/Pages/InformationServicesInterns.aspx)

AT&T Internships (http://att.jobs/careers/college/internships/technology-internships)

HP Internships (http://h30631.www3.hp.com/careers/it-students-and-graduates-jobs)

Verizon Internship Program (http://www.verizon.com/jobs/campus_internships.html)

IBM Extreme Blue Internship Program (http://www-01.ibm.com/employment/us/extremeblue/)

Boeing (http://www.boeing.com/boeing/careers/collegecareers/ITintern.page)

Microsoft (http://careers.microsoft.com/careers/en/us/internships.aspx)

Target Technology Leadership Program (https://corporate.target.com/careers/college-students)

Comcast Technical Operations Internships (http://jobs.comcast.com/Campus-Programs/Internships-and-rotational-programs/Comcast-Internship-Program)

Dell Summer Internships (http://www.dell.com/learn/us/en/uscorp1/internships)

Dow Chemical Information Research Internship Program (http://www.dow.com/careers/programs/student.htm)

Intel IRISE Software Engineering Internship (http://www.intel.com/content/www/us/en/jobs/locations/united-states/students/internships/intel-early-internship-software-engineering.html)

Google Technical Internships (http://www.google.com/about/careers/students/)

Humana Specialized College Programs – Information Technology (https://www.humana.com/about/careers/college-programs/specialized-college-programs)

World Fuel Services Fast-Track IT Program (https://www.wfscorp.com/Fast-Track_IT_Program)

Oracle Product Development Internships (http://www.oracle.com/us/corporate/careers/college/intern-at-oracle/product-development/index.html)

John Deere Information Technology Internships (https://www.deere.com/wps/dcom/en_US/corporate/our_company/careers/students/college/college.page)

Allstate Technology Leadership Development Program (http://www.allstate.com/careers/students-and-new-grads.aspx)

Morgan Stanley Industrial Placement Technology Internship (http://www.morganstanley.com/about/careers/programs/articles/282955423.html)

Nationwide University Relations Programs (http://www.nationwide.com/about-us/careers-college.jsp)

Cigna Technology Early Career Development Program (http://careers.cigna.com/CIGNAPage.aspx?page=102)

Time Warner Time Warner College Associates Program (TWCAP) – Technology (http://www.timewarner.com/careers/areas-of-operation/internships)

Halliburton GOSelect Information Technology Internships (http://www.halliburton.com/en-US/careers/students-and-recent-graduates/internships.page?node-id=hgeyxtcl)

Publix Supermarkets Information Technology Internships (http://corporate.publix.com/careers/support-areas/internships)

Raytheon Information Technology Leadership Development Program (http://jobs.raytheon.com/en/career-paths/campus-recruiting/leadership-development-program)

Xerox IT Internships (http://www.xerox.com/jobs/internship/enus.html)

Altria Information Technology Internships (http://www.altria.com/
Careers/Student_Center/Internships/Pages/default.aspx)

First Energy Information Technology Internships/Co-Ops
(https://www.firstenergycorp.com/content/fecorp/careers/student_
opportunities/co-op_intern.html)

Kellogg Information Technology Internships (https://www.
kelloggcareers.com/global/grow-with-us/career-opportunities/career-
opportunities-students-new-grads.html)

Viacom Internship Programs (http://www.mtvncareers.com/
internships.html)

*Anadarko Petroleum Information Technology Summer
Internship Program* (http://www.anadarko.com/Careers/Pages/
InformationTechnology.aspx)

Texas Instruments Software Engineer Internships (http://careers.ti.com/
intern)

Oneok "The One to Work For" Information Technology Internships
(http://www.theonetoworkfor.com/~/media/ONEOK/Careers/
PositionProfiles/Recruiting%20Insert%20IT%202011.ashx)

Thermo Fisher Scientific IT Program (https://www.thermofisher.com/
global/en/about/careers/itldp.asp)

Western Digital FIT-U Electrical Engineers Program (http://www.wdc.
com/en/company/employment/college.aspx)

Textron Leadership Development Program: Technology (http://
www.textron.com/careers/growth-development/LDP-IT.php)

Ecolab Information Technology Undergraduate Internships
(http://www.ecolab.com/careers/learn-more-about/campus-
recruiting/undergraduate-internships)

Visa Tech and Engineering Internships (http://usa.visa.com/careers/
university-recruiting/undergraduates.jsp)

Devon Energy IT Internships (http://www.devonenergy.com/Careers/
Pages/Students.aspx#terms?disclaimer=yes)

Applied Materials Co-Op/Internship Program (http://www.
appliedmaterials.com/company/careers/intern)

Ashland Information Technology Internships (http://www.ashland.com/
careers/Students-and-Graduates)

Agilent Technologies Technology Internships (http://www.jobs.agilent.com/students/usa.html)

Actavis U.S. Internship Programs (http://www.actavis.com/careers/university/internships-and-programs/internship-programs)

Booz Allen Hamilton High-Tech Internship Programs (http://www.boozallen.com/media/file/BAH-internship-program.pdf)

6.5 US RECRUITMENT ORGANIZATIONS

Job recruitment websites that offer cybersecurity positions include:

- USA Jobs (https://www.usajobs.gov/; this especially refers to the above sections)
- Computer Jobs (http://www.computerjobs.com/gb/en/IT-Jobs/)
  - Dice (http://www.dice.com/)
  - Monster (http://jobs.monster.com/v-security-q-cyber-security-jobs.aspx)
  - Career Builder (http://www.careerbuilder.com/jobs/keyword/cyber-security)
  - Indeed (http://www.indeed.co.uk/)
  - Beyond (http://www.beyond.com/)
  - The Ladders (http://www.theladders.com/)
  - Vault (http://jobs.vault.com/JobSeeker/Jobs.aspx)
  - Simply Hired (http://www.simplyhired.com/k-united-states-jobs.html)
- Glassdoor (http://www.glassdoor.com)

Here is a list of recruitment companies that specialize in cybersecurity job placement:

Alta Associates
Bartles Corner Rd, Suite 21
Flemington, NJ 08822
P: 908-806-8442

Benchmark
1984 Isaac Newton Square, Suite 202
Reston, VA 20190
P: 703-728-8506

Blackmere Consulting
3790 Founders Pointe Drive
Idaho Falls, ID 83406
P: (208) 932-2750

Coalfire
361 Centennial Parkway
Louisville, CO 80830
P: 303-554-7555

CT Partners
875 15th Street NW, Suite 901
Washington, DC 20005
P: 202-730-7905

Evan Scott Group International
1050 Connecticut Avenue, 10th Floor
Washington, DC 20036
P: 202-842-0441

LeznerGroup LTD
5140 Main Street, Suite 303–120
Williamsville, NY 14221
P: 212-920-6155

L.J. Kushner and Associates LLC
36 West Main St., Suite 302
Freehold, NJ 07728
P: 732-577-8100

Pinnacle Placements
132 Marlborough Street, Suite #3R
Boston, MA 02116
P: 415-495-7170

Radiant Recruiting
2435 North Central Expressway, Suite 1200
Richardson, TX 75080
P: 972-437-2777

Security & Investigative Placement Consultants LLC
7710 Woodmont Ave #209
Bethesda, MD 20814
P: 301-229-6360 or 301-424-1099

SecurityHeadHunter.com
POB 620298
Oviedo, FL 32762
P: 301-229-6360 or 301-424-1099

SecurityRecruiter.com
P.O. Box 398
Woodland Park, CO 80866
P: 301-229-6360 or 301-424-1099

Secure Recruiting International Inc.
3510 N San Miguel Street, Suite 111
Tampa, FL 33629
P: 813-258-8303

Cyber 360 Solutions
607 North Avenue, Suite 15–2
Wakefield, MA 01880
P: 781-438-4380

Potomac Recruiting
2200 Wilson Blvd. Suite 102–121
Arlington, VA 22201
P: 703-535-3133

CHAPTER 7

Interview Hacks and Tips

7.1 PITCH YOURSELF LIKE A CYBER PRO BY ASKING THESE QUESTIONS

We have established that while the United States is in dire need of more trained cyber professionals, there is a need for qualified and experienced personnel, so in this section we take a look at some suggestions to pitching yourself to maximum effect.

Great candidates ask questions they want answered because they are also evaluating the organization and deciding whether they really want to work for the company that is interviewing them.

Here is a selection of questions you can use in your next interview:

1. What do you expect me to accomplish in the first 60–90 days?
   Why ask this question? You will come across as very specific and detail orientated.

2. What are the common attributes of your top performers?
   Why ask this question? It sets you up as wanting to be a great long-term employee. Every organization is different, and so are the key qualities of top performers in those organizations.
3. What are a few examples of what drive results for the organization?
   Why ask this question? This will illustrate to the employer that you want the organization to succeed because he or she will also succeed as well.
4. What do employees do in their spare time?
   Why ask this question? Generally speaking, a happy employee likes what they do and like the people they work with. Unless the company is really small, all any interviewer can do is speak in generalities, but at least it shows that you want to fit in to the organization.
5. How do you plan to deal with...?
   Why ask this question? Every business faces a major challenge: technological changes, competitors entering the market, shifting economic trends, and so forth. So while you may see your first break in cybersecurity as a stepping-stone, you should still hope for growth and advancement. And if you do eventually leave, you will want it to be on your terms and not because you were forced out of the position.

7.2 HAVE ANECDOTES READY

Remember to have a few anecdotes ready. Having a short amusing or interesting story about a real security incident or a hacker will add color and personality to your interview. Here is an example of a social engineering "story":

"....One of my friends who works for a large cybersecurity firm told me about a clever Social Engineering Hack that actually took place. So, the hacker wants to place a RAT on an organization's network, so what he does is, he puts a suit on, prints off a fake resume and spills coffee all over it! He then walks into the organization he wants to hack and, all flustered and out of breath, talks to the girl at the reception and says:

"Hi....I'm so sorry to ask this! Can I ask you a huge super-massive favor! Can you please print off my resume!? I spilt coffee all over it and I have an interview at ABC Organization [which is located in the next building] and I'm already late! I really need this job and I don't think I'll be able to find an Internet Cafe in time to print off my resume....please, you'd really help me out! Please? I have the resume on my USB stick here..."

So, the receptionist, knowing how difficult the economy is these days and how tough the job market is, takes his USB Stick and pushes it into her desktop and prints off his fake resume and wishes him luck. He thanks her profusely knowing that he just infected their network with his RAT..."

7.3 BE AWESOME TO THE RECEPTIONIST!

This is so simple that anyone can do it and it will have a positive effect. Be very polite and try to create a positive impression with the receptionist. When you enter the building to say that you have arrived for an interview, the receptionist will ask for your details to confirm your time and meeting, and so forth . Make him or her feel comfortable and try your utmost to create a positive memory in their mind.

The reason for this is that it is likely that the interviewer and receptionist know each other and share experiences of who walked into the interview. If you have befriended an influence maker (the receptionist), then you have just jumped ahead of the pack! It works!

7.4 ORGANIZE INFORMATIONAL INTERVIEWS

An "informational interview" is an informal meeting you would organize with a cyber professional in which you ask them questions about how they started their career. These types of meetings are excellent ways to both learn about the skills required to land the entry-level position (or migrate into a security role) – and you never know; you might impress the person so much during the informational interview that they decide to offer you a job!

CHAPTER 8

Suggested Beginner and Intermediate Cybersecurity Training and Certifications

8.1 RECOGNIZED PROFESSIONAL CYBERSECURITY CERTIFICATIONS

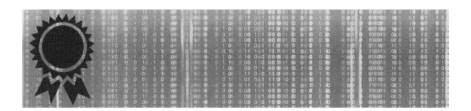

While many within the community argue the real benefit of professional training, one fact remains certain: Employers prefer experience over certifications.

8.1.1 Benefits of Certification

However, let us briefly look at the benefits of formal cybersecurity certification.

- Certification shows your commitment to learn industry standards, protocols, and methodologies.
- Certification allows you to join a membership body, which is great for networking.
- Certification requires continuing education that will force you to stay abreast of emerging threats and trends (vital in the security industry).
- Most professionals have a certificate of some description, so not having one will not leave you behind.
- HR managers often look for candidates with certifications.

In summary, getting a recognized IT security certification can only help and will likely contribute to your career. Here are our recommendations for beginner- and intermediate-level courses:

Beginner level:

- CompTIA A+
- CompTIA IT Fundamentals
- MTA: Microsoft Technology Associate: Database Fundamentals

Intermediate level:

- APT L1: Applied Penetration Tester Level 1 (Concise-Courses.com)
- CompTIA Security+
- CompTIA SMSP: Social Media Security Professional
- CCNA Security: Cisco Certified Network Associate Security
- CCIA: Citrix Certified Integration Architect
- CHFI: Computer Hacking Forensic Investigator (EC Council)
- GCIH: GIAC Certified Incident Handler (SANS)
- GISP: GIAC Information Security Professional (SANS)
- GSEC: GIAC Security Essentials (SANS)

8.2 BEST SCHOOLS FOR CYBERSECURITY

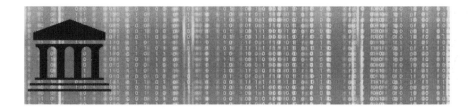

If you are thinking about studying in the United States, then consider schools that have been vetted by the NSA (National Security Agency) and the DHS (Department of Homeland Security) as "National Centers of Academic Excellence In Information Assurance."

On the basis of an in-depth study by the Ponemon Institute,[1] here are the results of the most highly rated cybersecurity schools in the United States. (The rankings are based on high scoring points in: academic

---

[1] 2014 Best Schools for Cybersecurity: Study of Educational Institutions in the United States, February 2014.

excellence, practical relevance, experience, and expertise of program faculty, experience and background of students and alumni, and professional reputation in the cybersecurity community).

- University of Texas, San Antonio (Texas)
- Norwich University (Vermont)
- Mississippi State University (Mississippi)
- Syracuse University (New York)
- Carnegie Mellon University (Pennsylvania)
- Purdue University (Indiana)
- University of Southern California (California)
- University of Pittsburgh (Pennsylvania)
- George Mason University (Virginia)
- West Chester University of Pennsylvania (Pennsylvania)
- United States Military Academy, West Point (New York)
- University of Washington (Washington)

8.3 SCHOLARSHIP OPPORTUNITIES

There are several scholarship programs in the United States. These include:

- *CyberCorps Scholarships by US Gov* (https://www.sfs.opm.gov/)
- *Scholarship for Women Studying Information Security (SWSIS)* (http://swsis.wordpress.com/)
- *Women's Scholarship from (ISC)2 Foundation* (https://www.isc2cares.org/scholarships/womens-scholarship/)
- *Undergraduate Scholarship from (ISC)2 Foundation* (https://www.isc2cares.org/Scholarships/undergraduate_scholarship/)
- *Graduate Scholarship from (ISC)2 Foundation* (https://www.isc2cares.org/scholarship/graduate-scholarship/)
- *AFCEA Intelligence Scholarship for Undergraduates* (http://www.afcea.org/education/scholarships/undergraduate/cyber-intelligence.asp)
- *NSF Programs for Undergraduates* (https://www.nsf.gov/funding/education.jsp?fund_type=1)
- *ADVANCE for Increasing Women's Participation in Sciences* (https://www.nsf.gov/funding/pgm_summ.jsp?pims_id=5383&org=ACI&from=home)

- *Information Assurance Scholarship Program (IASP)* (http://dodcio. defense.gov/TodayinCIO/InformationAssuranceScholarshipProgra m%28IASP%29/About.aspx)
- *Stokes Educational Scholarship Program* (https://www.nsa.gov/ careers/opportunities_4_u/students/stokes.shtml)
- The SMART Program (https://www.nsa.gov/careers/ opportunities_4_u/students/undergraduate/smart.shtml)

CHAPTER 9

Summary

9.1 WRAP UP AND SUMMARY

In summary, owing to the cybersecurity "skills gap" you have made a wise career choice!

To summarize, what we have outlined in this book, we see two vital and determining factors that will assist you in being able to land a job in cybersecurity, these are:

1. *Experience*: Although hiring managers are acutely aware of the shortage of cyber professionals, they are equally aware of the importance of hiring experienced individuals. If you lack experience, then we encourage you to either take a paid or unpaid internship, or, offer to audit and test friends and families business websites, computer systems, and networks; this in itself can be counted as experience and you can certainly place this on your resume.
2. *Knowledge, Skills and Abilities*: You must keep learning new technologies and applying them. A cybersecurity professional working in the field is only as attractive as the knowledge, skills, and abilities they possess. You must make yourself as attractive as possible by constantly learning new penetration-testing methodologies and processes.

We wish you the best of luck in your job search and hope that you enjoyed reading and learning from our book as much as we enjoyed writing it.